MW01043587

SWIMMING TO OBLIVION

SWIMMING TO OBLIVION

laura manuelidis

poems

CONTENTS

I

BROOKLYN IN MY BONES

STREET PERSPECTIVES

IN TRANSIT

II
INTERROGATIONS

ALTERNATING TEMPI

OUTSIDE TERRITORIES

WITHOUT CURE

III
UNDIMINISHED

QUANTA

A PURSE OF POSSIBILITIES

A POCKET OF SUSTENANCE

FINIS

"Hot sun, cool fire, tempered by sweet air,
Black shade, fair nurse, shadow my white hair."

George Peele

PREFACE

Subject: Checking in
Date: May 4, 2020

Laura you are a great poet!

I decided to read your poetry differently this time to try an understand your art better. I had three different readings and goals. The first time I noted what I felt, saw and heard. Next, a day later I asked myself what I remembered and lastly I looked at your craftwork to see what tools you used. Why? Because I don't know a lot about poetry and sincerely want to provide you with feedback that is useful.

At the first reading of _Restless_ I saw the city and sparkling windows. I felt the city's gravitas and it made me happy.

I was resistant to _Unfinished Paintings_ because I felt immediately biased towards liking the title so I put up my guard. This poem was very tactile and emotionally provocative for me.

Lastly, _Without Money_ made me think of loneliness and the loving mirror presented by dogs.

Later, I simply asked myself what I still remembered. This is from someone who misplaces things by nature. I remembered these fragments, "Granite and Sequins". These two words unlocked countless images and emotions I felt when looking at the city at night. Granite is heavy and permanent and sequins are light and flashy. That contrast captures the complex visual image and emotional meaning I experience when looking at the nightscape in two words. Brilliant.

I remembered "Floating its curves southward" I felt motion. I felt water dancing like a human and movement in a purposeful direction. This is sensuous and lovely. I saw the Hudson in my mind. The notion of a "Journey further than death" made me very uncomfortable. I knew what it meant on first reading but then I had to ask what does this really mean and what are all of the ideas I would have to forget and accept to understand this idea? That made me afraid and mortal. The "sly brush of circular reasoning" also made me feel uncomfortable because you prefaced that with waiting to be better or for me it meant reaching dreams. I felt worried that with key words like Unfinished, Sly and Circular you were sending a powerful message that outcomes and plans exist on two separate planes. So this was my favorite poem because it challenged me in many ways. Lastly "Crawls through my being" Wow. Those words truly express a defining type of love. It is complete, absolute and total.

I told you I studied your structure. I hate to confess, but my experience with poetry was during my sophomore year (1976) with a teacher who loved Walt Whitman. I remember my professor's words about structure, economy, context and rhythm (I wish I could go back and thank all of my teachers....I am sure they must have thought I did not care or wasn't listening at times).

I see your precision and craft. It's remarkable. I am beginning to see the depth, meaning and how your poetry encodes a universe. After our conversations in NYC this is a great artistic journey for me because you are my reference point.

cont.

All is well on the Left coast. I am working on a new painting. I will send a photo in about two weeks. I found an old picture of great uncles from the 1920-30's that I am using as my source. I am focused on art, keeping informed and staying healthy.

Sending you good energy and best wishes.

Kevin

NOTE ABOUT THE PREFACE:

The preface is a letter from a Los Angeles painter, Kevin Lance Daniels whom I met in February 2020 at the Whitney Museum's marvelous opening of "Vide Americana: Mexican Artists Remake American Art". We were both spending a long time looking at *"Hombre y Mujer"* by Rufino Tamayo.

So we began a true friendship, and continued to converse by cross-country email about painting and cities, sharing some of our works in progress. Here is his spontaneous reaction to the last 3 poems I sent him from this book. His comments mean a great deal to me because they are about substance and shared ways of how we may all speak with each other. Only the typeface is changed.

LM

I

BROOKLYN IN MY BONES

STREET PERSPECTIVES

To Brower park in Brooklyn

Snow whispers across the cheeks.
Snow falls lightly on the stars
Collects and collapses.   Or,
        depending on the night—
Pirouettes—before it flits beyond the lamppost.

Unseen, the children trek deep tunnels of snow
        one blizzard winter night
        to arrive at the end of streets:
The beginning of the park
        and its castle, now locked
        with electric trains that never broke:
The world ignoring signs to stop.

Perhaps there's a full moon
        waltzing behind the drifts
        piled higher than our heads.
Perhaps there is nothing.   Or,
        less than nothing, an imaginary *i*
        skipping below the surface:

cont'

The *i* no one listens to
    now in its quietude again
Rediscovering night's illusions
    frozen in the brain:
The original sensation
    of being one with the cosmos—
Swirling and speechless.

Walk-up Brooklyn

i.

An empty coat hanger: The long hall.
Splinters catch the foot.
Doors close for undeliverable messages
Of war.
The smell of cabbage.   Always sour.

Electricity flicks erratically every
Frozen evening
–Uninvited–
Descends the stairs.

Sewing machines force
Needles up & down.
A treadle with ornate metal curls keeps
Clanking beneath the moon
Overlooking
A nameless field of broken mechanisms:

Metal and bones.
The messiness of earth's
Buried placentas.

cont.

ii.

One first grows up bargaining for life,
Two shoes for January's ice
Polished by the Lower East side
For the scuffs of real Amerika—Forgotten—
Determined.   Courageous.   Desecrated
Under fancy stores filled with mannequins
Still clutching furs
On thick summer days.

It's always a challenge
To visit the old neighborhood—its crease of time—
Or recognize a single soul who held your hand.
A couple of people know you by your eyes.
A few others smile.

On the burnt stoops of Pacific Street
Narratives continue to flutter
Between the cardboard fans, the sweat,
A blade or two of grass: Fenced in.

The shops on Nostrand Avenue
Where the trains stop
Continue to
Display something under glass
No one can afford.
Like the TV we used to crowd around outside.

cont.

iii.

Impossible to contain the then
Now useless trolley tracks nearby, their flattened grooves
Rattling across the intersection of working
Cherry bombs.
The deadly accident.   Sirens too late.
The soft conversing that vanished between the flutter
Of days
Along with being free to roam like a small pea anywhere
Unseen
Under a neighbor's shadow.
Just another mistake around the next corner:

No lights, no cameras, no poking microphones.
No interviewers in white plastic masks
After the pistol shots, when the street is being cleared
Repeatedly asking, just in time for the evening news,
Really,
How it feels.

Other offspring
(for Bessie Calhoun Gantt)

Likewise, I am a 5 cent pleated fan
Torn within
Your chariot of arms
Swung low
    through the midnight stars promising release:
    trapped on a rutted road in chains

    while in the Calhoun common room
His white name elevates his portrait.
Even the sound of his name
Suffocates the amber touch of your skin
    as other people read aloud about the wounded stag
    discussing the impossible problem of translating:
"The meek and bleeding flower".

This leads me to the cement stoops
    of Brooklyn summers:
Aunt Eloise recounting her own
Stories of the railroads
Persistent as the slow sweep of her fan.

cont.

I must remain silent here
For my references are all wrong
While you continue to caress the matchsticks of my ribs
    with rightness
    (never rebellion).

I am still promising
    to release your breeze of freedom—
Your only child—
    in this shackled land.

Calhoun college, Yale, 2002

Around the corner

In the oasis of Brooklyn I came out:
  then rapidly crawled back in, an embryo.
Who was I to confine love to the nipples on my chest?

I came out of the snake, speaking not evil.
  I arrived with my small carved idol cleverly hidden.
"Throw it away, Rachael—they said—

Bury its evil pockmarks beneath your hood:
You will be stamped with an eternally insignificant symbol
Everyone recognizes."

I felt something else: —my desires—
Confusing me, plucking their own mysterious melodies.
(I had not yet been introduced to the dissonance of love).

I watched the symmetry of bodies sauntering before me
  on an ancient street of immaculate nakedness
Where small gods are always entering.   And suddenly disappearing

Around the corner——   within the strays of forbidden light
One finally sloughs off the old admonitions
  and suddenly morphs into the visible: A woman.

Genesis 31: Rachael hid her father's small idols under the camel cushion and
told her husband Jacob she could not rise up because the "way of women"
was upon her. Unaware, Jacob cursed with death whoever stole them.

The play never ending

He washes himself thoroughly
        in rustled waters
As he prepares his restless mount
        for more vagabond days.

By accident.   Or by fate
He comes to my far-away village
        with his well-trained Gypsy stallion
Pawing the ground
        —& graciously bowing—
Before he creates one incomplete circle
For escape.

His tragic, large eyes bring me dazzling presents,
        so many, that I do not recognize myself
Transformed by his vision,
        or the rapidly sliding mercury
Inflaming his songs.

These quicken my desire
To have him
        come inside me
                Unspeakably.
: He pauses.
        And obliges.

cont

So I have begun to understand him
    this beautiful pickpocket child
Shaped by the passing wind
    whose face I drink as morning
        Nestles under my palms.

At the edge of the garden

The donkey I used to laugh at
Took me up the mountain:

Not that animal with perfect even teeth.
Not that Arabian with rounded hard cheeks
    whose sweat becomes perfume
    between my thighs
Irresistible in stampede
    with his stallion snort that continues
    to paw my admiration
Kicking up ancient dust from my always present
    Landscape.

        No:

Not that one who abandoned me
When I had no water left in my womb:

Only my darling donkey lifted me up the mountain
    of my mistakes
    so many that she whinnied for them
Nibbling the poppies   : encouraging the evening
Apple to shine blissfully.   I watch her small, left deft hoof now
    As it steps over the crevasse.
    Also her outsized head, always quizzical.

No wonder the Arabian of my first dreams
Wants to mate with my silly donkey.

Intermittently

My brother told me how to watch the watch
The second hand introducing hidden short episodes.
He stashed his faith on the shoulders
Of a pasture:

My brother showed me how to negotiate
Beside the river wandering to its salted mouth:
To place my small footsteps carefully
While grazing.

My brother led me out of the streets
Raining with light that obliterates sanity
As he shielded me from foreign onslaughts
I deserved:

My brother—and his shadow—around the next corner
Always protects me.

IN TRANSIT

One day

We all strode in as adolescents
Under the gothic arch with Greek letters about torches bearing flames.
We took off our shoes, undressed in separate bathrooms,
    the men and women
Put on our greens (now blues),
Scrubbed beneath our fingernails with harsh bristles
And drenched our forearms
Vertically, moving the long curved silvery release of water with our
    elbows bent
Before inserting our hands into the gowns
And then the gloves that still allowed some feeling
Through the glass door, inspected, then opening.

It was not much different from the first day
We split it in two, the sternum, to hold the dog's stray heart
Beating, beating, beating: beating vigorously still
Glowering.   Until we put it to sleep–
Its pound of existence–for the last time
Abandoned on the street.

Late now, in the glazed existence
Where the winter solstice barely lights my bathroom.
I try to escape my face in the mirror.
I brush my teeth and see the trickle of toothpaste
Down my forearms that I still raise
Vertically beneath the imaginary
Bent handle that commands the faucet to open.

cont

Once, perhaps, I could stop or start in the past
Of unfortunate diagnoses.
I do nothing for no one now with what I know.
Just walk the emptied streets.

Veterans where have we sent you?

We love all our children playing war games inside:
Such exuberant birds
    spectacular, wild and loud,
Unfettered by our monochromatic pride

While on 25th just east of 8th
Now sick and confused
Some thing that once resembled a man
    in a ripped khaki coat
    with an insignia patch from Vietnam
Attempts to stand—
Foot bones and the bones of his hand sticking out—
    and other parts naked
Unable to pull up his beltless pants.

One colored woman, walking by
    with the help of a cane, in her black polished
    cleaning lady shoes
Quietly slips a five dollar bill in his pocket.

But how will he fight this impassable ice
    in the shadow of a crack doorway
Confabulating next spring
When the poppies regrow
    the shade of new blood.

(blocks of ice, NYC, Feb. 2014)

Undocumented

You may not think they are the same:
The bodies in imaginary blankets under the flapping green awnings
Someone forgot to roll up this Christmas tree evening
    for the snow.   The soft immersive snow

You may not think they remain:
The bowery veterans clasping their voluminous pants
Still wiping your windshields through the 20 second red light
    after you exit the old bridge from Brooklyn.

You may not think they managed to survive:
These left over children whose mothers and fathers
Slipped in from somewhere else, with never enough money
    for a school lunch, or peanut butter for the jelly sandwich.

You might not think about how this then became the
Emptied factories, with workers lingering outside in assembly lines to
Bring home some food for negligible wages.   Or the coal miners
    with the soot of black labor coating their alveoli.

You might not think about anything if you have helicopters waiting to
    take you to another island, another continent, another nameless
Planet, anchored to an exclusive ladder that elevates only the chosen
Above the moon: Beyond the clutch of compassion.

        (Kol Nidrei, 2019
)

The exile

Just checking in.   Raining here today
Came home 5 minutes ago.
Leftover steak in the fridge.

Whad'ya do today?
Would be good to hear from you sometime.
The weeds are way overgrown—the driveway—
Needs a new mowing machine.
Lots of repairs to do
Just to keep up
My non-appearances.

Cats walk the wires overhead sounding
Hungry:
Robbins almost gone.
The old smell of smoke in the chimney
Curls up through the grate—and slowly
Evaporates above the blue evening.

Just checking in.
Can't really tell you on the edge of my bed
How it feels
Hooked up

cont.

To these newfangled breathing contraptions
Always clicking and beeping so
I can't sleep.

Tomorrow will check in again.
Should I tell you the first story you used to love
About the garden that always grew up
To meet the fell of light

Until it blossomed silences.

In the distance

The child is naked
Running with pail and shovel up the shore
    to catch the flight of plovers
Bomb diving above his head.   And the gulls
Plunging into the swirls of bluefish
Snapping at everything, breaking the surface photons
    that keep skittering across the bay.

The tardy elders watch old joy renewed, and anticipate
Dismay, as foam seeps slowly around the sandcastles
    left behind last night
Transfiguring the aperture of time.

But the young care only about the present:
Another chance to build something more magnificent
    as they greet each uncharted day of summer with its curious
First kiss
Sailing up the incoming foam.

What was that day about that slipped
    above away
Into swift sheets of nothingness?

We tuck old people in their places

Always perfectly arranged
    under white tablecloths with military folded corners
And small silver spoons.

Better to pass by as part of the crowd
    to survive.
Better to blend in
    and smile synchronously with the iridescent
Reflections on the spotless pool.
Or to mate with whomever is left over:
    another crumb of toast
Pecked, packaged and emaciated.

Better just to plug in to some analog foreign songs,
Gypsy overtones, irreverent wedding dances.
Pretend they're what's currently playing so unpleasantly
    on the intercom under the domineering videos.

Not a good idea to ever admit
One is adrift in the primal cave of Plato,
    wandering with Wordsworth on the walk,
    modulated by the light of JS. Bach
Or understanding—the perfect imperfection of death.

(last visit to Geoffrey Hartman

Her Kind
(alternate version of Anne Sexton's)

I have chosen self-erasure for a long life.
Served tea and pizza in a dump.   Always fired
For talking to the patrons.   Tips: I had no
Interest in.   Just the books in corners
Clasped by cobwebs.   & the smell of dying
Flowers as they fell after pollinating summers:
A good act.

I have chosen to disrupt my rarified class
By stating the obvious.   This reminds
Them of their stinginess.   I have worn
Sneakers to shreds that are then most comfortable
& completely unfashionable, as my white hair now
Shouts the flaming insurrection of small kindnesses:
A good act.

I have chosen my body to script
All its inherited languages, already parsed
For a tomorrow that will
Scale ignorance for the fabulous experiences
Witten by the universe of photons
Piercing the cell of love.   Others know this IS:
A good act.

Spring again with Mrs. Nobody

i.

at the post office:

> I sent a letter to inform
> Someone

else

> Who has no address
> About what others call

not death

ii.

meanwhile

> Behind the window
> Mrs. Nobody replies:

you need

> To make up your mind
> To open the door extravagantly

to go

> Outside
> Where the sun's lost photons

recombine.

Without money

I will purchase a dog who will love me
    and bark like the stars, unconditionally
When I return from my squish of sullen sod
To remind me how lucky I am
    to be smelled and recognized by my deepest orifices
    and afterwards, tugged back to city curbs for comparison.

Dog sits at my feet
    as cat climbs most cunningly on my chair of myths.
Dog asserts itself as a corporation growling,
Challenges intruders surveying its beloved territory—
    while cat, aside, slides between my thighs
    its secret, conditional love.

Beyond cat and dog, an unpossessible beast I most respect
Crawls through my being

Five classmates:

WHO is going to kill the dog?

Not I

Not I

Not I

Not I

Not I

After long hiatus

Good to come back to this autumn evening:
Its copper blues vibrate with the bass note
    of a low-hung moon.
From the top of the dunes all tides recede
    their joyous morning greetings disparu.

Time to wonder why we are still alive
    while others did not continue.
What would they have done in our places?
What would they have created
    to join our odd, stained windows?

We see through different eyes now, more patient,
Having negotiated a long journey   accidentally
    wandering into uncertain wisdom
One can speak of only to children
    who realize the beauty of nature's imperfections

Always in view, always ignored.
I would like to crown this moon's bald calvarium
    with the last chromatic leaves falling from the faces of my friends:
Unimportant personages who tried to build and leave
    the whole world glimmering.

II

INTERROGATIONS

ALTERNATING TEMPI

Pause

Midnight within the red rose of midnight
Shadows the abandoned desk.
Thin rectangular sheets, still unwritten
Hide other sheets, incessantly reciting, underneath.

Their white wings emerge as butterflies
To beat the sun's rays before dawn.
In perfect 4-fold symmetry, mirrored inked spots
Interrogate the elastic horizon of time:
Time that is nothing without its author—

A cigarette ash—
Drifts from the lip of a word

Not allowed to be spoken.

Restless

I turn off my lights to peer
Into this city that refuses
       to close its electrified eyes

This center: our city
Stacking its granite
Dressed up in sequins again

       to solicit the unknown.
A siren concatenates, and then diffuses
The pointed origami of time.

Rapt with oil and balms

The priest circles his tomb
Waiting for one star to penetrate
His narrow channel.

Flowers on both banks of the Nile, in parallel
Open their parched arms
For the glorious sound of flooding.

In the telescopic room
Contemplation anticipates eternal bliss:
Walking hieroglyphs temper their pacing

While on the muddy tributaries boys swirl their poles
Until old men arrive in their mirror of water, looking out.
Weirdly the flowers smile.   And vanish in small eddies.

In the youth of ontogeny
Some almost perfect structure reassembles
Individual fingerprints, embedded longings.

Unfinished paintings

of evening
before the dive into night
that accentuates our tinseled
necklace crossing the Hudson:
Floating its curves southward.

Night with its ice islands
lists through this winter
as the stars, overhead
chart another journey outward:
Further than death.

How long will we wait
to become better than we may be:
Touching up our windowless projects
with the same sly brush of
circular reasoning.

OUTSIDE TERRITORIES

No trespassing

Migrating on wind
    the butterfly of ideas assembles the earth's terrain
        via two unblinking and jubilant eye-wings:

A perfect, symmetrical target for the darts of its jealous enemies
    clad in barbed wire,
        posting their pride-warnings
            to reject any challenge to their territories.

Butterfly ignores the obedient bugs who always
    creep together in armies, banging their chitin,
        advertising their own bizarre dung marketplace
            where everything is sold.
                Until nothing remains

Except butterfly, who manages to soar past corrupted theorems
    to greet the nascent meadows
        concatenating imaginary numbers
            plucked from a stillness that moves beyond time

Isis on the wall

On her white wall
shadows of torn leaves storm.
Attack the vertical
joints of our wood-crossed
       Windowpanes.

Shapes can't find their margins.
The trumpets sound confused
while the back ward insane
try to re-buckle their straightjackets from behind.
       Detritus seeps through floors.

On the flaking, whitewashed wall
a narrative flits by;   it's garbled notes
inspire Scheherazade to twine her voice once more
around the cuneiform decree that coalesces each night
       Before her final sacrifice.

In the basement, cobwebs and statues clash.
Lurid, dismembered videos now play
       Raucous and broken jazz.

Isis: Goddess who shelters the weak and births the cosmos.

Trespassed

Here she stands in a moving film
Recording the downcast
Rubble of concrete posts

Bearing the frayed
Sounds of her language – how she says mother–
Rubble of the human home.

Now she knots her shawl
As she inhales another day from broken pots:
    "I beseech you, with your oiled steam

Whistling through the cracks in my clay
To stop the bombs, the fires eating us:
Which way can one turn?"

Swaddled in black cloth
Stars have no freedom to annotate her space.
Where is the future dromedary to carry her
With only a crumpled tablet of dates?

"Sometimes I envy the dead": she says.

2015: Glimpse of Syria from a combat transport

Another day, 2015

So sad the end day
The end of one day, this day
Before the sun is laid again
Upon its bed in colored disarray
Calling us to listen to the taps
For soldiers.   And their prey.

A giant surging tear forms now
And stays inside.
One hears the cantor's son
His last day dressed in uniform
His larynx bulleted mid-song:
Sing now for him:

It takes some courage also
For the imam on a trembling tower
To start his chant again tomorrow
When behind him
All is rubble.

The women of the village
Wrap their infants
In their ragged shawls
Wandering to find the place
Where innocence—somewhere—
May wake.

today's obituary from Iraq

Frankincense

No calligraphy can entwine a mind
    longing for the East:
        Light always rising.

Nature's mace, its spikes of light
    once smote each core, but now finds not
One shred of love unburnt
    beneath our smothering cities.

When I attempt to return with an ineffable companion
    in the guise of a flower or an insect
Nothing greets me except metallic shapes,
Glowerings of lost petals, and delicate
    the detached wings
Lacking the amber fragrances
        Of the once living

East exquisite, now a storm of dust
    Converted.

Beyond the fence
Idomeni, Greece March 2016

The children fled as uprooted wildflowers.
They dispersed between the pale flax of morning
    bent by the north winds:
The rhythm of time
Syncopated.

The children sped
        with dried blood crusting their memories:
Flimsy colored petals.

Underneath the tent
Dampness turned into a mud basin
Deeper than the thigh of a 4 year old with arms raised
    but holding flowers
Already rotted.

Look at the beautiful faces
    of these children
Playing like lion cubs
Harmlessly kissing each other
    under blankets
Tasting the sweetness of new saliva   And
Imagining a flawless

Tomorrow

When I was a child

When I was a child I spoke as a child.
When I was a woman I whispered as a child

to the child bandaged, with his bloodied mind
Holding his hand out to me

while examining me intently with closed eyes.
His eyes the eyes of his mother and his father

still searching for our neglected understanding.
Matted in sweat, why does this child

Lend me permission to do anything to him?
A surrender without surrender

Accepting the sunrise departing the horizon.
Nothing could save it:

It—   was once so beautiful.

2018, January

It is not a good year.
I am freezing and the paper news
Stands upright to salute
While the globe rotates.
Evil—of a common type—
Aggravates our days.

Everywhere one looks
There is want, but no mercy.

We study bottles of rotted anatomies
Harvested from the frayed earth.
I drink—real alcohol—
When I come home from work.

Only the owl hoots.

Immigrants

Love the zebra:
Love the hoofbeats of his heart
Escaping its stripes.

Watch the wings of dragonflies
Crackling as glazed glass
In the choirs of an evening sky

Or rain, that lands the flanks of petted cows
Who moo for grass—now
Slippery under hoof.

Glint of snow, under sun, under moon
Changes as love does—all
Phases combine.

Then why block our admission
Of orphans locked in trucks
          with their waiting, crowded eyes?

Interlude of new space

We wander through the poverty of a desert.
Not a palm visible.
No fate traceable.

With tapering fingers
We seek the old silk route, crossing sands
Swept by incurable curved shadows.

Cast between alternating stars
Too numerous to guide us through this frozen
Night— with its flashing, distant planets

Two women spread their dyed red carpets
To receive the guests at a time before.
Momentarily, the wind quiets.

We wander incessantly to find another lifeform to join
As if there shall always be something vital.
We enter a swirl of seas embraced by the emptied Nautilus.

WITHOUT CURE

Wheat fields with cables

The train is going somewhere.
I hear its red hoot.
Doves scatter:
Then reassemble on my roof.

They build a nest of light
From strands of my white hair
And nestle their faded eggs in rafters
To retrieve the organic past

That lives only in a painting
Composed before the floods and ash:
Printed green promises now exchanged
For a barren internet.

Irretrievable

Hidden within the dying coral reefs
The vanishing swarm of ideas
May yet survive as dreams
Swimming through their bleached lacunae.

No dreaming fish sway here:
Their currents of pleasure fouled.

Everything of our small earth today
Records a synchronous decay,
A zero of the thick green kelp
Where once Cetacea milked and played.

Now earth suspends in negative time
As a sailor lost
Without his ancient syllabus
Of uncorrected stars.

Electrocardiogram

This relative train ride never stopped.
Some of us hurtled forward, some forgot

our limited time, that once appeared: Absolute.
Only one sextillionth of a cosmic second separated us

from the vast, ceaseless storms raging far out
as we broadcast our passions and our beliefs—

whatever might magnify our existence—
Even the irregular tracings of our flailing hearts.

Some crave power.   Others succumb
to the run around the sonic laugh of light

That never travels without its shadow.

Without cure:

A closed window.
A prison of ghost birds.
The altar prisoner looks mournful
Inside his ornately carved wooden frame
    Its iron latch a perpetual
    Winter of Saturn.

Incessant detentions, instantaneous
Judgements, straightjacket our house.
It makes one insane.
I walked up the echoing stairs
    To the locked wards
    Where no doctors came

Played chess on the walls
Squared by shadows—shivering light—
With Chekov a lost book, wearing his number 6.
Along the corridor, not even a dream:
    Only the stench of too many drugs
    In the urine.

The cutting

Whoever is my jailer
Is the jailer of the flower.
He tears off my petals
With the heel of his boot
　　and grinds them on aggregates of concrete.

He hangs me upside down—
Assisted by a withering bitter woman—
To collect the dust of my saffron
So that it's delicacy
　　can never be savored again.

She quarters my stem slowly with an endless string
　　of dental floss from heaven
Excruciating my silence.

They continue to suffocate my fragrances
In centuries of ignorance
　　so the sons will be manly as death.
And always victorious.

The men in Médecins sans Frontières gave sterile razors
to the women who cut female children.

Violence

The wild boar jumps up to kiss me
The one with his coat of thick, sharpened bristles
Perfectly aligned.

I turn my face aside—somehow thrust him off
This one last time.   Nothing remains of my history
To drain.

The bedside light—faint and desperate—
Vilifies
The stars.

The ICE Jackets

Another march subpoenaed me last evening
    after I succumbed to the solitude of old age.
I turned around: Faced my emptied ghost.

My papers were already executed: And my crime?
Forgotten stars leapt from night's narrow crevasse
    where mother moth tucks in her eggs

Sewing her stories together with red thread.
I always waited in my bed.   This night—
    out from under the covers—my history escaped.

Over my shoulder crawled the hideous punctuated
    transformation of Kafka I became at 13.
I was in Prague, a few blocks from the clock tower

Dissected on a biblical window, half-underground, naked.
Across the street: shattered headstones, alphabets in flame.
It's late.   Now, some Other must inherit my star.

ICE : US Immigration and Customs Enforcement

Wave beyond C minor

I was swaddled in a swell, face down.
Asleep with the sea.
Hours passed.   Or was it days?   Or generations
    waiting for the dawn.

How long had I been dreaming?
The wind between two dunes
    started to modulate its keys.
Sparse plugs of grass played
Only one overtone.

My mother and my husband were running toward me.
Or was it my father?   Or the three in a row
Leaning over the guardrails
Waving hello.   And then waving more furiously
    motioning to come home.
Only silence surrounded me.

I was fine I tried to tell them.
Awake now.   And smiling.
I merely had drifted, taken
    by a current more rapidly than I realized
Down the shore, and further out than I thought.
Far out
    beyond the point.

cont

Don't worry I shouted back
    —as if they could hear me—
I'm a very strong swimmer

        Though I can't lift my arms
to reach you
        From beneath these heavy covers.

Serendipity

A broken branch suddenly juts out
        from the sand-bright beach I wander.
Gulls squawk: Too late in the season now for hawks.

Stroking its frozen chronology of famished seasons
        this wood splinters my mind.
Its Cyclops knot of eye, mottled and damp
        stares back at me: An infidel.

I pack it under my armpit.
Trudge home to meet my empty hearth
        where nothing melts.

I turn it upside down so it can examine me
        as I am: Another species.
Sometimes I flip it over to its blind side.
But it follows my pacing
        as the shadow of my mother.

Once I laced three emptied seashells around its neck
        to hear it amplify the bitter harmonies of winter winds.
Another time, I painted a turquoise sky on bricks for it to soar.
But that was a sedentary space: My fabrication.

cont.

I even balanced it high on a Lucite pedestal
        so it could inspire
Tomorrow's gold light's shavings.

Why does it keep interrogating me?

As if I can cure death.

Before the final impediment

I loiter wherever I am led.
My path chooses me.
I pretend—
I have somewhere to go.

My watch face betrays me:
Its irritating
Blinking eye.

I tread on the fallen:
Heavy stars.   Their memories
Betray this day's
Cerulean sky.

With infinite alternatives before me
I contemplate only pebbles
Not unsurmountable stairs.

After copious night sweats
I babble a stream
Of colorless sounds
Drifting in go-no-place time.

Cosmic Ecology

Yearning returns to the emptied nest,
Its brambles still perfectly arrayed
    to roughly fit the abandoned egg:
A shell whose contents flew away
    within one breath
Escaped.   And dazzled day.

Where, now, are its lovely flutterings and vital songs
    that congregate our rounded earth—
Collaborators of joy and pain that we force senseless now
    into the cold, indifferent hole of time
So every species is collapsed and made invisible
    as tiny immobilized elements of our most base designs.

And will these recombine & then erupt a new planetary nest?
Companion to the one we so foolishly destroyed.

III

UNDIMINISHED

QUANTA

Rejoice for quintessence

It grows from nothing
Visible.

It snakes between the grasses
Overflowing with blinding might:

A shadow
Consuming its own silence,

Meandering
Through every crevice of the cell

Too statistically devious
To be collected

Or brusquely:
Apprehended.

One:

A Blessed woman walks
    toward the counsel of light.
Obstructs no one.   Rests on a broad dais of palms.
Composes a desert of faint cinnamon:
Delight for the nameless
    Being in everyone

    VISIBLE
As each of her offspring planted in a cloud
Shapes its own fruit original
    with unpredictable precision
Perpetually singing from the core of common seed— safe
    Beyond withering

    WIND
Drives the forgotten ones into winter's ground to wait
    for the return of her mothering—
Plains dampened for plenty.
They refuse barrenness and judgments:
    Scorch of her tributaries.

    ENERGY
Returns to matter—reigniting the spread of joy
    green and flowering—
Before our time concatenated.
This heals our shattered earth and its
    Every loneliness:

One must endure this famine we begat
    For her offspring

Recall for dawn

Tonight, the spires of stars
Trap a doe
In their fading webs of light

      the one with handsome flanks, &
Delicate shoulders: Her neck
Not tense or arched.

Her eyes mirror
The bouquet of morning
I am about to walk into

      the beginning of my abode
Where stag also gathers
Day's sleek manifestations.

Curiously, I closed my eyes
So that you might come back once more
Before leaping

      a tint of sage in blue flower
Beyond the encroaching
Transparency

Sand

In the coherent white glare of tomorrow
it becomes hard to remember what you said under the
    Canopy of foam.

Saying goodbye, a filigree of moans
blankets this earth, as each human grief, never complete
    Slides from day:

Day that always promises the blossom of re-becoming
purple, translucent and calm: some hidden passerine
    Going nowhere

while suddenly, deep in the leaves, he clears his warbling
wherewithal to send his polished song aloft
    To be revealed

in a chromatic someday that surely must be perfect:
A place where one again can dream the imperfect
    Life lived

together, unpossessed inside one grain of chance
that can't ever catch the logical bus to school
    Entering the unknowing.

Camel sayings

I will lead you out of heaven in its loneliness,
Unknot the red handkerchief
    that drinks the thick sweat of your thinking:

I will unpack your burden of judgement
    and release the explosion of your spices:
Short days of fragrances.

You will nuzzle the curve of this earth
    as my brother's equal sister
And nibble its nascent harmonies, a refuge beyond oases.

Your snort will perpetrate the puff of love
    through winter's domed tabernacle
Rested and liberated:

I will lead you out of your confinement—
    those old and opaque blue pigments—
Into a canvas of transparencies, vistas without calendars

As seed leads the camel forward.

A PURSE OF POSSIBILITIES

Once again:

Seeking an inlet from the winds, their howling
    worse than the cats tonight in heat coupling.
Seeking refuge in a cave
    with only stalagmites for canes.
Seeking not an absolute truth but its shadows
    never stationary
Before they slip away.

Unable to know what we did with our lives
    but vaguely comprehending, one suddenly becomes elated
Passing through this space with our youth in full display,
    as in these granular sepia prints
Barely recognizable now, but still
    embedded in our brains
Until our small day ends.

Windswept

By now I can tell the gulls from the hawks
    between my thin kite lines
    that hold my dreams afloat

By now I notice the small details of the thick shouldered
    herring gull from those that peck at sand in the Carolinas
    where my son & his wife nested for a while

By now I know there are ways to distinguish one type
    from another: by their black or white markings,
    their relative poverty or plenty.   And also

By now I feel their clime through the drift of rapid squalls:
    an arbitrary compress of time
    that mutes each labored song.

By now I have played out every possibility
    of who I am with all my brother and sister
    windswept species.

Hurricane called Irma,
Sept 8 2017

I am doing nothing on my birthday
while one son battens his arms against the winds

that excavate the shiftless tides separating him
from his wife and children whom he sent, last night, away.

One cat is sick, irreparably
seeking the last of sun in which to lay

to den its straying warmth before some arbitrary fate
rides over the man-made barriers of concrete arrogance.

Money will not stop the faceless sea of souls crying out
about injustice, or the ceaseless arguments

& apprehensions crawling up our shores
through the inert lines of gasless cars

Favoring only the small gods on their hoods in dry garages.
As if they would defend and preserve us.

Free of Jonah's Judgement

I enter a zip code of paradise.
It reveals the geography of my personal weather on a spider's web.
Dew crawls down its threads, accentuating today's forecast:
Scattered undertows, nodular storms in my sea, this rich Atlantic

      where whales recover from winter by rupturing the sky
Proffering songs I can't translate, so imprecisely moving.
Just 80 feet offshore now, my squint of sun
Deciphers their surface krill and calcified periwinkle shells.

—I thought they were almost mating: —No. Just showing off
      for the vast horizon that traverses their sonar souls
Lusting the waves—slapping them to foam
Across the soliloquy of our temporary borrowed swells

In time with the shore

I have seen the water ease into a strange calm.
Have seen the water rage
    and sailed its wings of foam without fear.

Now, as I amble—no home in sight—
    my antediluvian brain
Follows these shrunken shores that reflect
Only a static, crystalline.

What if the rains reappear
    (& when shall they come back?)
Will the visionary eagle recover
    from its hovering extinction?
Or the field mouse guide the dead again
    deep inside its burrowed domains—
Or the sunstroke goat lick our hands for salt,
Or the vulture winds that winter through our house all year
Recall the truest songs

Imprinted by fossil bones
    and painted in the caves of art
Where all the species dance.

At last

To express more than I see
    is my purpose.
To pull the blanket of childhood
Under the chin of frost that now
Sprouts only thick black hairs of age
Until the soft white plume of forgetfulness
Descends my screen
    for sleep.

I mean by that
    our species' end:
The end of also elephants
Their carcasses without tusks.
I mean the ant
Set fire to and smoking on its heap.
I mean each leaf
Scraped by the loneliness of our streets
Abandoned by its half molted caterpillar
Who tries to fly away
    as if he can escape
The lethal iridescence
Spreading overhead.

To offend these invisible slow
Accumulating events that make us fragile
I borrow words.

A POCKET OF SUSTENANCE

Magic

Through the dream
Impossible to tear apart
A child came
As dew on the bone.

The yesteryear of webs
Guided her slide, perfectly calm.
Nothing flew overhead.

In wetness submerged
The last page of the world
Unfolded its original smile:
So the woman began.

Your cheek is my pasture

Every day is most beautiful before dawn
Even as it hides below the fog
Briefly resting on the marsh—
      Oboe sounds in grass
      Bending to the touch of early warmth

The bulk of mammals still asleep
Voles in their digs
Birds becoming sensate to their branch:

An easeful time
When only Jupiter and Venus remain
To wrestle in the ring
      The nocturnal umpire moon already heavy and low
      Falling under the lid of scattering light

While other early days—when no thoughts clutter the sky—
Catch whatever wisps of wind slide by
Barely audible:

cont

Yes, I will miss these summer times beside the cheeky chipmunk
Chewing my pines still plump and green on tree
Who flies off at my invasive cries—as if
     I were not with him—
     Feasting.

Words now have their first curfews as the light
Changes costumes in this haze of heat
By 6 AM inducing me again to sleep

While fox on dune, unguarded, smiles
At the sudden plethora of butterflies,
And horseshoe crab, armored by the past
     Silently tracks the wet sand by the dry
     Always caught between the more—Indefinite tides

Where small dog in the galaxy
Rests his nose between the disappearing paws of night
And lion meekly steps aside

     For morning's rise

Feb 2014 NYC, ice encasing everything:
How the mind survives

And so I entered the forgotten world

At ease

I go to school at night
Because light
Violates my vision, alters my recall.

I go to school every night
To relearn the immensity of the universe;
To lie down on the pointed tips of tall cypresses

Just to contemplate the clarity of darkness
Until the bottomless bottom quark escapes
To join the future to its shadow.

Up and down the ribbons of time that last our pages
Miniature summers reappear, blooming as perpetual petunias
Beside a river shedding silver fish that leap through our blood:

Imaginary projections of accumulated wisdom.
Over the horizon I go nowhere beyond
Because night becomes itself, self-fulfilling

As beauty does in the final shade after our sunsets
Where the crickets slow down for autumn, and then lapse,
Evening plaintive, the transparency we call sacred overtaking.

*bottom quark, also known as the beauty quark, always entangled

FINIS

Acknowledgements

The author is indebted to Deepti Pradhan, a colleague at Yale with meaningful knowledge that extends through science, music and poetry. Her most thoughtful questions led to several good changes in the manuscript before publication.

I am also grateful to the editor of the *"Innisfree Poetry Journal"* (Issues 21, 23, 25, 28, 30) for kindly publishing sets of poems from this book, the editor of *"Night Picnic"* (Vol. 1 & Vol. 2) for publishing other sets of poems from this book, including one in a bilingual Russian translation, and to the editor of *"Grey Sparrow Press"* for publishing *"Rapt with oil and balms"*.

The manuscript's typeface is Bodoni 72

About the Author

Laura Manuelidis is a physician who is also known for delineating large chromosome domains by their DNA motifs and curvature. Her scientific contributions to late onset dementias, particularly human Creutzfeldt-Jakob Disease and similar infections, are less appreciated. She has published two previous books of poetry: *"Out of Order"* and *"One divided / by Zero"* , and her poems have been published in diverse literary magazines including *"The Nation"*, *"Evergreen Review"*, *"Oxford Poetry "* and *"Innisfree Poetry Journal"*.

About the Cover

The sculpture is by Mary Frank, born in London, 1933, who lived with her grandparents in Brooklyn for a time, studying at the Brooklyn Museum of Art School where the author used to sled — all of us on cardboard sleds—down the back hill while our parents were painting. Mary Frank was essentially self taught, with no formal training in sculpture. She has been referred to as *"the visual poet of the inner life"*. This sculpture *"the swimmer"* was on display at the Whitney Museum in New York. The photo and cover were made by the author.

ISBN: 9781651416563

Made in the USA
Middletown, DE
04 June 2020